D0593568

THE WORD BECAME FLESH AND
MADE HIS DWELLING AMONG US.
WE HAVE SEEN HIS GLORY.
THE GLORY OF THE ONE AND ONLY,
WHO CAME FROM THE FATHER,
FULL OF GRACE AND TRUTH.

—JOHN 1:14

Presented:

to: _____

_____

_____

by: _____

_____

on: _____

_____

The
CHRISTMAS
STORY

from the family reading Bible

ZONDERVAN®

The Christmas Story
Copyright © 2010 by Zondervan

The Holy Bible, *New International Version*®
Copyright © 1973, 1978, 1984 by Biblica, Inc.™
All rights reserved

Published by Zondervan
Grand Rapids, Michigan 49530, U.S.A.

www.zondervan.com

Library of Congress Catalog Card Number 2010930452

Printed in the United States of America   NIV 6/11/2010

10 11 12 13 14 15 16 /DPM/ 15 14 13 12 11 10 9 8 7 6 5 4 3 2 1

ABOUT
THE CHRISTMAS STORY

The Christmas season is a very special time for all of us. We say it is a time for family, a time to draw closer to one another and a time to build and share memories that will last a lifetime. But often, the Christmas season becomes cluttered with to-do lists, activities, shopping, decorating and all the hectic ways in which we "celebrate" the holiday season. You may crave something different. You may wish your family could slow down, quiet down and discover the true meaning of the "holy-day."

Take heart, the Advent and Christmas season can be more meaningful for you and your family—a season for growing sturdy spiritual roots, roots that are planted in the rich soil of God's Word. To help you do that, we have designed this little book. It is both a Bible study and a devotional book with which your whole family can dig a bit deeper into the story of Christ's coming.

Twenty readings reveal the whole story of God's grace in sending Jesus, our Savior to live on earth and walk among us. Each reading includes a Scripture passage—actual words from the *New International Version* of the Bible. The readings also include interactive features, questions and explanations that will help your family delve into the meaning of the readings. These readings will challenge your family to think about the "big picture" of Jesus' coming to earth as a human being, experiencing life as we do and becoming one of us. But you will also discover more and more that he is the one true God, the Messiah, whose coming, which brought salvation to all humankind, was predicted long before it happened.

There are seven readings from the Old Testament that cover the prophecies and some background about the

Messiah's coming. The next eight stories relate the events immediately surrounding and including Jesus' birth. The final six readings show how Jesus is the Son of God and how Jesus has made God's love and forgiveness available to every one of us. As a result, you and your family will follow and understand the story of Jesus' birth as you never have before.

Explanation of Features
Included With Each Reading

Just the Facts are straight-forward questions with concrete answers. A verse reference follows each question so you can easily find the specific answer. Some of the questions are designed to be easily answered by younger children; some are harder to provide a challenge to older children.

Let's Talk questions are intended to encourage discussion. These questions are not necessarily connected to a particular verse. There may more than one "right" answer. Some are open-ended and have no "answer" at all, but are there to help you and your children think about what God wants you to learn from the story that's been read. Some of these questions may be too difficult for young children. Feel free to skip them if you wish.

Why This Matters underscores the core message of the passage and will help you answer the question that kids often ask: "Why do I need to know this?"

Points of Interest highlight something surprising or little known about the passage. This might be a cultural insight, a geographic or archaeological fact, a historical note or a fun detail. From time to time it may explain a puzzling aspect of the passage.

Tips for Parents

- Do the best you can to have devotions regularly with your family, but don't feel guilty if you miss sometimes. With today's busy schedules, many families find it difficult to have a family devotional time every day.

- Every family is different. You may find that a slightly different structure to your devotional time than that suggested here works best for you. Feel free to adapt this information to the needs of your family.

As Mary watched her child Jesus grow, "in wisdom and stature," she "treasured all these things in her heart" (Luke 2:51–52). As you and your children share God's Word during this Christmas season, may you all grow in wisdom and may you "treasure in your hearts" these blessed times you spend together.

TABLE OF CONTENTS

A BRIEF HISTORY
OF GOD'S PEOPLE

The Bible tells many stories about the history of God's people. If you'd like to know more about these stories, you can find them in the *Family Reading Bible*. Check it out! In the meantime, here is an overview to give you some background for *The Christmas Story* from the *Family Reading Bible*.

Long, long ago God told a man named Abram (later called Abraham) to travel to a new country. He didn't tell Abraham why or where he was supposed to go, but Abraham had faith in God, so he packed and went. After Abraham had traveled a long way, God brought him to the land that would become his own. God told Abraham that he would make his family great and that his descendants would be as numerous as the sand on the seashore. To prove it, God told Abraham that he and his wife, Sarah, would have a son. They were old and it seemed impossible, but Sarah got pregnant, and their son, Isaac, was born.

When Isaac grew up, he married Rebekah, and they had a son named Jacob. When Jacob, who was also called Israel, grew up, he had 12 sons, and his sons each had large families. God was faithful to this family. He took care of them and remembered the promises he had made to Abraham.

Because of a famine, Jacob and his sons and their families and animals went to live in Egypt. Over time, they had more children and their families grew very large. Because Jacob's descendants, now called the Israelites, were so many, the Egyptians became afraid of them and made them their slaves. Jacob's descendants served in Egypt for many years, and they had to work very hard.

How they suffered! They asked God to get them out of Egypt and out of slavery, so God sent a man named Moses to help them. God sent plague after plague to convince the king of Egypt to free the Israelites. Finally a day came when the king told Moses, "Leave my people, you and the Israelites! Go ... Take your flocks and herds, as you have said, and go" (Exodus 12:31–32).

Moses led the Israelites on a journey out of Egypt and to the land God had promised to their ancestor Abraham. Sometimes they obeyed God on the journey, but sometimes they didn't. When they disobeyed, God disciplined his people. Because the Israelites disobeyed God, they wandered in the desert for 40 years. Still, God did not forget them; he provided water and food for them.

After Moses died, another leader, Joshua, led the people into the land God had promised them. There, each tribe was given land of its own. God gave the Israelites many laws and commandments for living holy lives that would be pleasing to him. Sometimes the people didn't do what God asked (that is called sin). God appointed Levites, members of one of the Israelite tribes, to serve him and to make sure the people worshiped him correctly and reverently. Some of the Levites were appointed as priests. Because of the Israelites' sins, the priests offered animal sacrifices to God so they could be right with God once again. But the people kept sinning, so the sacrifices had to be made over and over again.

God loved his people and wanted the very best for them. But to be blessed by their holy God, they had to live holy lives and follow God's rules. God wanted to be number one in their lives, but the people were often tempted to worship false gods. When they fell away from God, he sent leaders called judges to get them out of trouble. The judges told the people what God wanted them to do. Often the judges were military leaders who led the Israelites to victory over their enemies.

Because the nations all around the Israelites had kings, the Israelites wanted a king too. God warned them that it wouldn't work out well for them, but they insisted. God appointed a king named Saul. But Saul decided to do things his own way, so God took away Saul's power and made a shepherd boy, David, the son of Jesse, Israel's king. David, though he wasn't perfect, had a heart for God. Through David, God continued to keep the promise he had made to Abraham. And that's where the story of Christmas begins.

David's Forever Kingdom

King David loved God and wanted to build a temple for God to live in. But God said he would establish an even greater "house" — a kingdom that would last forever. God had great plans for David's family. Not just for his son or grandson, but for someone who would be born many generations later.

2 Samuel 7:1-17

GOD'S PROMISE TO DAVID

7 After the king was settled in his palace and the LORD had given him rest from all his enemies around him, ²he said to Nathan the prophet, "Here I am, living in a palace of cedar, while the ark of God remains in a tent."

³Nathan replied to the king, "Whatever you have in mind, go ahead and do it, for the LORD is with you."

⁴That night the word of the LORD came to Nathan, saying:

⁵"Go and tell my servant David, 'This is what the LORD says: Are you the one to build me a house to dwell in? ⁶I have not dwelt in a house from the day I brought the Israelites up out of Egypt to this day. I have been moving from place to place with a tent as my dwelling. ⁷Wherever I have moved with all the Israelites, did I ever say to any of their rulers whom I commanded to shepherd my people Israel, "Why have you not built me a house of cedar?"' '

⁸"Now then, tell my servant David, 'This is what the LORD Almighty says: I took you from the pasture and from following the flock to be ruler over my people Israel. ⁹I have been with you wherever you have gone, and I have cut off all your enemies from before you. Now I will make your name great, like the names of the greatest men of the earth. ¹⁰And I will provide a place for my people Israel and will plant them so that they can have a home of their own and no longer be disturbed. Wicked people will not oppress them anymore, as they did at the beginning ¹¹and have done ever since the time I appointed leaders*a* over my people Israel. I will also give you rest from all your enemies.

"'The LORD declares to you that the LORD himself will establish a house for you: ¹²When your days are over and you rest with your fathers, I will raise up your offspring to succeed you, who will come from your own body, and I will establish his kingdom. ¹³He is the one who will build a house for my Name, and I will establish the throne of his kingdom forever. ¹⁴I will be his father, and he will be my son. When he does wrong, I will punish him with the rod of men, with floggings inflicted by men. ¹⁵But my love will never be taken away from him, as I took it away from Saul, whom I removed from before you. ¹⁶Your house and your kingdom will endure forever before me*b*; your throne will be established forever.'"

¹⁷Nathan reported to David all the words of this entire revelation.

---

a 11 Traditionally *judges*   *b 16* Some Hebrew manuscripts and Septuagint; most Hebrew manuscripts *you*

JUST THE FACTS

1. Who gave God's message to King David? (v. 4)
2. What did God promise his people? (vv. 10 – 11)
3. What did God promise David and his descendants? (vv. 12,15 – 16)

LET'S TALK

1. What do you think it meant in David's time to "establish a house"? In what ways are families important in our culture today? How is your family important to you?
2. Who were your ancestors? How many generations can you identify? What is it like to imagine having children and grandchildren who will come after you?

WHY THIS MATTERS

God made a promise to David that he would establish a kingdom for David's descendants. Hundreds of years after David died, God sent his Son, Jesus, who came from David's family, to be the king of the Jews.

POINTS OF INTEREST

7:6 The "tent" God was referring to was the tabernacle that had been his portable dwelling place ever since the Israelites camped at Mount Sinai in the desert. It was intended to be used only while the Israelites were on the march. But the Israelites had lived in the land God had promised them for more than 400 years and still had not built a permanent temple — a house in which they could worship the one true God.

The Sign of Immanuel

Years after God made the kingdom of Israel great through King David, God's people were again disobedient to his laws and commandments. The nation of Israel became divided into two: one country was called Israel and the other was called Judah. So God sent messengers, called prophets, to announce his words to the people. Isaiah gave this prophecy first to King Ahaz of Judah when his country was about to be invaded by the armies of Israel and Aram. The king was fearful; he was not trusting God to take care of him and his country. The prophecy was fulfilled a short time later when a young woman, who may have been Isaiah's wife, became pregnant (Isaiah 8:3–10). But the prophecy was also fulfilled much later when another young woman, Mary, became pregnant (Luke 1:26–38).

Isaiah 7:10 — 8:10

[10] Again the LORD spoke to Ahaz, [11] "Ask the LORD your God for a sign, whether in the deepest depths or in the highest heights."

[12] But Ahaz said, "I will not ask; I will not put the LORD to the test."

[13] Then Isaiah said, "Hear now, you house of David! Is it not enough to try the patience of men? Will you try the patience of my God also? [14] Therefore the Lord himself will give you[a] a sign: The virgin will be

[a] 14 The Hebrew is plural.

with child and will give birth to a son, and[a] will call him Immanuel.[b] [15]He will eat curds and honey when he knows enough to reject the wrong and choose the right. [16]But before the boy knows enough to reject the wrong and choose the right, the land of the two kings you dread will be laid waste. [17]The LORD will bring on you and on your people and on the house of your father a time unlike any since Ephraim broke away from Judah—he will bring the king of Assyria."

[18]In that day the LORD will whistle for flies from the distant streams of Egypt and for bees from the land of Assyria. [19]They will all come and settle in the steep ravines and in the crevices in the rocks, on all the thornbushes and at all the water holes. [20]In that day the Lord will use a razor hired from beyond the River[c]—the king of Assyria—to shave your head and the hair of your legs, and to take off your beards also. [21]In that day, a man will keep alive a young cow and two goats. [22]And because of the abundance of the milk they give, he will have curds to eat. All who remain in the land will eat curds and honey. [23]In that day, in every place where there were a thousand vines worth a thousand silver shekels,[d] there will be only briers and thorns. [24]Men will go there with bow and arrow, for the land will be covered with briers and thorns. [25]As for all the hills once cultivated by the hoe, you will no longer go there for fear of the briers and thorns; they will become places where cattle are turned loose and where sheep run.

ASSYRIA, THE LORD'S INSTRUMENT

8 The LORD said to me, "Take a large scroll and write on it with an ordinary pen: Maher-Shalal-Hash-

---

[a] 14 Masoretic Text; Dead Sea Scrolls *and he* or *and they*
[b] 14 *Immanuel* means *God with us.*   [c] 20 That is, the Euphrates
[d] 23 That is, about 25 pounds (about 11.5 kilograms)

Baz.[a] [2] And I will call in Uriah the priest and Zechariah son of Jeberekiah as reliable witnesses for me."

[3] Then I went to the prophetess, and she conceived and gave birth to a son. And the LORD said to me, "Name him Maher-Shalal-Hash-Baz. [4] Before the boy knows how to say 'My father' or 'My mother,' the wealth of Damascus and the plunder of Samaria will be carried off by the king of Assyria."

[5] The LORD spoke to me again:

> [6] "Because this people has rejected
>   the gently flowing waters of Shiloah
> and rejoices over Rezin
>   and the son of Remaliah,
> [7] therefore the Lord is about to bring against them
>   the mighty floodwaters of the River[b] —
>   the king of Assyria with all his pomp.
> It will overflow all its channels,
>   run over all its banks
> [8] and sweep on into Judah, swirling over it,
>   passing through it and reaching up to the
>   neck.
> Its outspread wings will cover the breadth of
>   your land,
>   O Immanuel[c]!"

> [9] Raise the war cry,[d] you nations, and be shattered!
>   Listen, all you distant lands.
> Prepare for battle, and be shattered!
>   Prepare for battle, and be shattered!
> [10] Devise your strategy, but it will be thwarted;
>   propose your plan, but it will not stand,
> for God is with us.[e]

---

[a] 1 *Maher-Shalal-Hash-Baz* means *quick to the plunder, swift to the spoil*; also in verse 3.   [b] 7 That is, the Euphrates
[c] 8 *Immanuel* means *God with us.*   [d] 9 Or *Do your worst*
[e] 10 Hebrew *Immanuel*

JUST THE FACTS

1. What did God want Ahaz to do? (7:11)
2. What was the sign God promised to send? (7:14)
3. What was the boy going to eat? (7:15)

LET'S TALK

1. This prophecy was meant for Ahaz's time, but it was also a foreshadowing of Jesus' coming. Why do you think the prophet gave two meanings to these verses?
2. "Immanuel" (7:14) means "God with us. " When do we use the name "Immanuel" today? Can you think of a song about Immanuel?

WHY THIS MATTERS

The sign God gave to Ahaz — a virgin giving birth to a son and naming him Immanuel — is a key promise about the coming of Jesus Christ. When Jesus came to earth, God really *was* with us.

POINTS OF INTEREST

7:15 The land was devastated by the Assyrians, so there was no harvest. The people lived on anything they could find on the land. What they found was curds and honey; these two items refer to a simple diet of natural foods. Curds were a kind of yogurt.

A Child Is Born

This passage is another part of the prophecy Isaiah gave to Ahaz, the king of Judah. The Assyrian Empire was threatening to take over the lands that surrounded it. Isaiah warned the people about the destruction that was to come to Judah. God's nation, it appeared, would be torn down, but it would not be dead forever. Isaiah's prophecy is not only about his own time but also about a time far in the future.

Isaiah 9:1-7

TO US A CHILD IS BORN

9 Nevertheless, there will be no more gloom for those who were in distress. In the past he humbled the land of Zebulun and the land of Naphtali, but in the future he will honor Galilee of the Gentiles, by the way of the sea, along the Jordan—

²The people walking in darkness
 have seen a great light;
on those living in the land of the shadow of death[a]
 a light has dawned.
³You have enlarged the nation
 and increased their joy;
they rejoice before you
 as people rejoice at the harvest,
as men rejoice
 when dividing the plunder.
⁴For as in the day of Midian's defeat,

[a] 2 Or *land of darkness*

27

you have shattered
　the yoke that burdens them,
　　　the bar across their shoulders,
　　　the rod of their oppressor.
⁵Every warrior's boot used in battle
　　　and every garment rolled in blood
　will be destined for burning,
　　　will be fuel for the fire.
⁶For to us a child is born,
　　　to us a son is given,
　　　and the government will be on his shoulders.
　And he will be called
　　　Wonderful Counselor,ᵃ Mighty God,
　　　Everlasting Father, Prince of Peace.
⁷Of the increase of his government and peace
　　　there will be no end.
　He will reign on David's throne
　　　and over his kingdom,
　establishing and upholding it
　　　with justice and righteousness
　　　from that time on and forever.
　The zeal of the LORD Almighty
　　　will accomplish this.

ᵃ 6 Or *Wonderful, Counselor*

JUST THE FACTS

1. What event was coming? (v. 6)
2. What are some of the names this special child would have? (v. 6)
3. How long would this king reign? (v. 7)

LET'S TALK

1. What is it like when everything is dark? What about when someone turns on a light? How does this news bring people out of "darkness" and into "light" (v. 2)?
2. This child would have several names. What does each of them mean to you? Discuss each one.

WHY THIS MATTERS

Though God's people were facing a frightening enemy, God did not let them face the enemy without a message of hope for a glorious future — a time when they would live in peace, prosperity and joy.

POINTS OF INTEREST

9:1 The land of the tribes of Zebulun and Naphtali became the land of Galilee. When Jesus began his public ministry in Galilee, he fulfilled Isaiah's prophecy recorded in verses 1–2.

God's People Ask for Salvation

This psalm, or song, was written as a prayer to God when the nation of Israel was torn apart by a foreign nation, probably Assyria. God's people had to flee from their homes and farms. They suffered many hardships. They longed for God to send someone to save them from their enemies and restore their nation. At this time, God's people described the nation as a vine that had been planted but had now been trampled and burned.

Psalm 80:1–19

PSALM 80

For the director of music. To ˌthe tune ofˌ
"The Lilies of the Covenant." Of Asaph. A psalm.

¹Hear us, O Shepherd of Israel,
    you who lead Joseph like a flock;
you who sit enthroned between the cherubim,
        shine forth
²   before Ephraim, Benjamin and Manasseh.
    Awaken your might;
        come and save us.

³Restore us, O God;
    make your face shine upon us,
    that we may be saved.

⁴O LORD God Almighty,
    how long will your anger smolder

against the prayers of your people?
⁵ You have fed them with the bread of tears;
   you have made them drink tears by the
      bowlful.
⁶ You have made us a source of contention to our
      neighbors,
   and our enemies mock us.

⁷ Restore us, O God Almighty;
   make your face shine upon us,
      that we may be saved.

⁸ You brought a vine out of Egypt;
   you drove out the nations and planted it.
⁹ You cleared the ground for it,
   and it took root and filled the land.
¹⁰ The mountains were covered with its shade,
   the mighty cedars with its branches.
¹¹ It sent out its boughs to the Sea,^a
   its shoots as far as the River.^b

¹² Why have you broken down its walls
   so that all who pass by pick its grapes?
¹³ Boars from the forest ravage it
   and the creatures of the field feed on it.
¹⁴ Return to us, O God Almighty!
   Look down from heaven and see!
 Watch over this vine,
¹⁵   the root your right hand has planted,
   the son^c you have raised up for yourself.

¹⁶ Your vine is cut down, it is burned with fire;
   at your rebuke your people perish.
¹⁷ Let your hand rest on the man at your right
      hand,

^a 11 Probably the Mediterranean   ^b 11 That is, the Euphrates
^c 15 Or *branch*

the son of man you have raised up for
yourself.
¹⁸ Then we will not turn away from you;
revive us, and we will call on your name.

¹⁹ Restore us, O LORD God Almighty;
make your face shine upon us,
that we may be saved.

JUST THE FACTS

1. Where does God sit? (v. 1)

2. What did this writer ask for? (vv. 2–3)

3. What happened to the vine? (vv. 8–11,16)

LET'S TALK

1. Why do you think the writer used the word picture of a
vine? Why not just say "Israel"?

2. What did the people promise to do if God sent them a
ruler? (v. 18) What did they mean by saying they would
call on God's name and not turn away?

WHY THIS MATTERS

God's people continued to plead with God to show
mercy and save them. He answered this plea many
centuries later by sending his Son, Jesus.

POINTS OF INTEREST

80:1 Cherubim are a special kind of angel. They
were guardians protecting the way to the tree of life
in the Garden of Eden. They also protected the ark
of the covenant in the tabernacle and in the temple.
In this psalm they are said to guard God's heavenly
throne. Cherubim are described as having wings and a
combination of human and animal characteristics.

The Branch From Jesse

Sometimes after a tree is cut down, a new green shoot grows out of the stump. Jesse was King David's father, so the "stump of Jesse" (Isaiah 1:1) was Isaiah's way of referring to David's family. When the nation of Israel was divided and eventually destroyed, it appeared that David's family had died out. But God promised that a "shoot" would grow from it — a new leader would be born to give the nation hope.

Isaiah 11:1–10

THE BRANCH FROM JESSE

11 A shoot will come up from the stump of Jesse;

from his roots a Branch will bear fruit.
²The Spirit of the LORD will rest on him—
the Spirit of wisdom and of understanding,
the Spirit of counsel and of power,
the Spirit of knowledge and of the fear of the
LORD—
³and he will delight in the fear of the LORD.

He will not judge by what he sees with his eyes,
or decide by what he hears with his ears;
⁴but with righteousness he will judge the needy,
with justice he will give decisions for the poor
of the earth.
He will strike the earth with the rod of his
mouth;

with the breath of his lips he will slay the
  wicked.
⁵ Righteousness will be his belt
    and faithfulness the sash around his waist.

⁶ The wolf will live with the lamb,
    the leopard will lie down with the goat,
  the calf and the lion and the yearling*a* together;
    and a little child will lead them.
⁷ The cow will feed with the bear,
    their young will lie down together,
    and the lion will eat straw like the ox.
⁸ The infant will play near the hole of the cobra,
    and the young child put his hand into the
      viper's nest.
⁹ They will neither harm nor destroy
    on all my holy mountain,
  for the earth will be full of the knowledge of the
    Lᴏʀᴅ
    as the waters cover the sea.

¹⁰ In that day the Root of Jesse will stand as a banner
for the peoples; the nations will rally to him, and his
place of rest will be glorious.

---

a 6 Hebrew; Septuagint *lion will feed*

JUST THE FACTS

1. What gifts would the Spirit give this "shoot" (v. 1) when the Spirit rested on him? (v. 2)

2. What would the "shoot" wear as his belt? As his sash? (v. 5)

3. What animals are mentioned in this reading? How will these animals someday behave? (vv. 6–9)

LET'S TALK

1. Why do you think Isaiah talked about the Messiah's coming by using words about growing things, like the "Branch" and the "shoot" (v. 1)? What sometimes happens when you cut off a plant that still has deep, living roots?

2. What did Isaiah mean when he said, "The wolf will live with the lamb, the leopard will lie down with the goat" (v. 6)? What would life be like if the world was that peaceful?

WHY THIS MATTERS

God gave his people hope. He taught them to look for the Messiah by telling them what he was going to do long before it happened. Just as Israel looked for the Messiah, we can hope and look forward to Jesus coming again to bring a time when there will be no more violence or cruelty.

POINTS OF INTEREST

11:8 The cobra and the viper are poisonous snakes. The cobra, which can grow to eight and a half feet long, was the deadly Egyptian cobra, used in Egypt as a religious symbol. It is usually found on the north and east coasts of Africa, with a variation of the species located in the Arabian Desert. The picture of a child calmly playing near these feared reptiles was a sure sign that the Messiah would change everything.

God Will Come to Save

In another prophecy Isaiah said that the coming Messiah would heal people and perform other miracles. When Jesus came, he did all the things that Isaiah had talked about hundreds of years before.

Isaiah 35:1–10

JOY OF THE REDEEMED

35 The desert and the parched land will be glad;
the wilderness will rejoice and blossom.
Like the crocus, ²it will burst into bloom;
it will rejoice greatly and shout for joy.
The glory of Lebanon will be given to it,
the splendor of Carmel and Sharon;
they will see the glory of the LORD,
the splendor of our God.

³Strengthen the feeble hands,
steady the knees that give way;
⁴say to those with fearful hearts,
"Be strong, do not fear;
your God will come,
he will come with vengeance;
with divine retribution
he will come to save you."

⁵Then will the eyes of the blind be opened

and the ears of the deaf unstopped.
⁶Then will the lame leap like a deer,
and the mute tongue shout for joy.
Water will gush forth in the wilderness
and streams in the desert.
⁷The burning sand will become a pool,
the thirsty ground bubbling springs.
In the haunts where jackals once lay,
grass and reeds and papyrus will grow.

⁸And a highway will be there;
it will be called the Way of Holiness.
The unclean will not journey on it;
it will be for those who walk in that Way;
wicked fools will not go about on it.*
⁹No lion will be there,
nor will any ferocious beast get up on it;
they will not be found there.
But only the redeemed will walk there,
¹⁰   and the ransomed of the LORD will return.
They will enter Zion with singing;
everlasting joy will crown their heads.
Gladness and joy will overtake them,
and sorrow and sighing will flee away.

ª 8 Or / *the simple will not stray from it*

JUST THE FACTS

1. How would the desert and wilderness rejoice? (vv. 1–2)

2. What would happen to blind people? Deaf people? Lame people? (vv. 5–6)

3. What would be the name of the highway? (v. 8)

LET'S TALK

1. A "contrast" shows the differences between two things, such as the contrast between desert land and land that has plenty of rainfall. How many contrasts can you find in this passage?

2. Who will walk on the Way of Holiness? How do you picture this? What will it be like?

WHY THIS MATTERS

God promised that the Messiah's coming would change people in many ways. The Messiah would heal, perform miracles and bring salvation to everyone who believed in him. When Jesus the Messiah came, he brought a new kingdom into being.

POINTS OF INTEREST

35:1 The crocus mentioned here is not the early spring flower that we are familiar with. Rather it refers to the saffron crocus, a spring flowering herb used to produce saffron powder, which is used in cooking. This flower is fairly common in Palestine today.

The Messiah Will Come From Bethlehem

God gave Micah a message for the people of Israel: in their lifetime their nation would be destroyed. But God also gave Micah a vision of bright hope — with details! Micah predicted an important event in a little town in Judah that would make the town famous.

Micah 5:1-5

A PROMISED RULER FROM BETHLEHEM

5 Marshal your troops, O city of troops,[a]
for a siege is laid against us.
They will strike Israel's ruler
on the cheek with a rod.

[2] "But you, Bethlehem Ephrathah,
though you are small among the clans[b] of Judah,
out of you will come for me
one who will be ruler over Israel,
whose origins[c] are from of old,
from ancient times.[d]"

[3] Therefore Israel will be abandoned
until the time when she who is in labor gives
birth

[a] 1 Or *Strengthen your walls, O walled city*   [b] 2 Or *rulers*
[c] 2 Hebrew *goings out*   [d] 2 Or *from days of eternity*

43

and the rest of his brothers return
  to join the Israelites.

⁴He will stand and shepherd his flock
  in the strength of the LORD,
  in the majesty of the name of the LORD his
    God.
And they will live securely, for then his greatness
  will reach to the ends of the earth.
5   And he will be their peace.

DELIVERANCE AND DESTRUCTION
When the Assyrian invades our land
  and marches through our fortresses,
we will raise against him seven shepherds,
  even eight leaders of men.

JUST THE FACTS

1. What town was the prophet talking about? (v. 2)
2. What did the prophet say about this small town? (v. 2)
3. What would this ruler be like? (vv. 4–5)

LET'S TALK

1. What do you think it means that the ruler over Israel would be one "whose origins are from of old, from ancient times" (v. 2)?
2. How has Jesus' greatness reached to the ends of the earth? Discuss.

WHY THIS MATTERS

Christ existed long before history began. He was present at the creation of the world. Jesus will rule forever as our shepherd, giving us peace and security as our "Prince of Peace" (Isaiah 9:6). God chose the little town of Bethlehem to be Jesus' birthplace long before he was born.

POINTS OF INTEREST

5:2 Though Bethlehem was a small town, it had an important place in the history of God's people. Jacob buried his wife Rachel there (when it was called Ephrath, Genesis 35:19). Ibzan, a judge of Israel, was from this town. So were Boaz, the husband of Ruth, and David, who kept his father's sheep and was anointed king by Samuel. Modern Bethlehem is a small village of fewer than 10,000 people. The surrounding hillsides abound in figs, almonds, olives and grape vines. The shepherds' fields are located northeast of the town still today.

The Birth of John Foretold

Many years later, Israel came under the powerful rule of the Roman Empire. The empire ruled over the Jews and made them pay heavy taxes. They still longed for a savior to rescue them and restore their nation. The right time came for God to fulfill his promise and send the Messiah. But first he would send a special messenger to announce Jesus' coming and get the people ready to accept their Savior.

Luke 1:5–25

THE BIRTH OF JOHN THE BAPTIST FORETOLD

⁵In the time of Herod king of Judea there was a priest named Zechariah, who belonged to the priestly division of Abijah; his wife Elizabeth was also a descendant of Aaron. ⁶Both of them were upright in the sight of God, observing all the Lord's commandments and regulations blamelessly. ⁷But they had no children, because Elizabeth was barren; and they were both well along in years.

⁸Once when Zechariah's division was on duty and he was serving as priest before God, ⁹he was chosen by lot, according to the custom of the priesthood, to go into the temple of the Lord and burn incense. ¹⁰And when the time for the burning of incense came, all the assembled worshipers were praying outside.

¹¹Then an angel of the Lord appeared to him, standing at the right side of the altar of incense. ¹²When Zechariah saw him, he was startled and was gripped

with fear. ¹³But the angel said to him: "Do not be afraid, Zechariah; your prayer has been heard. Your wife Elizabeth will bear you a son, and you are to give him the name John. ¹⁴He will be a joy and delight to you, and many will rejoice because of his birth, ¹⁵for he will be great in the sight of the Lord. He is never to take wine or other fermented drink, and he will be filled with the Holy Spirit even from birth.ᵃ ¹⁶Many of the people of Israel will he bring back to the Lord their God. ¹⁷And he will go on before the Lord, in the spirit and power of Elijah, to turn the hearts of the fathers to their children and the disobedient to the wisdom of the righteous—to make ready a people prepared for the Lord."

¹⁸Zechariah asked the angel, "How can I be sure of this? I am an old man and my wife is well along in years."

¹⁹The angel answered, "I am Gabriel. I stand in the presence of God, and I have been sent to speak to you and to tell you this good news. ²⁰And now you will be silent and not able to speak until the day this happens, because you did not believe my words, which will come true at their proper time."

²¹Meanwhile, the people were waiting for Zechariah and wondering why he stayed so long in the temple. ²²When he came out, he could not speak to them. They realized he had seen a vision in the temple, for he kept making signs to them but remained unable to speak.

²³When his time of service was completed, he returned home. ²⁴After this his wife Elizabeth became pregnant and for five months remained in seclusion. ²⁵"The Lord has done this for me," she said. "In these days he has shown his favor and taken away my disgrace among the people."

ᵃ *15* Or *from his mother's womb*

JUST THE FACTS

1. Who was Zechariah? What was his wife's name? (v. 5)
2. Who visited Zechariah in the temple? What was the message? (vv. 11–17)
3. What happened to Zechariah? Why? (v. 20)

LET'S TALK

1. Was Zechariah's inability to speak a punishment or a blessing? Explain.
2. In what way would John "go on before the Lord, in the spirit and power of Elijah" (v. 17)? Why did the angel compare John to the Old Testament prophet?

WHY THIS MATTERS

God kept the promise he had made to his people through the prophet Isaiah. John was "a voice of one calling: 'In the desert prepare the way for the Lord '" (Isaiah 40:3). John preached repentance so the people could accept the Good News of Jesus.

POINTS OF INTEREST

1:5 Both Zechariah and Elizabeth were Levites and descendants of Aaron. Only men from the family line of Aaron could be priests. Groups of priests rotated serving in the temple. They presented sacrifices and offerings to God, taught and carried out God's laws for worship, maintained the temple, lit lamps and burned incense, and talked to God on behalf of the people of Israel. Zechariah was on duty and serving as priest when the angel came to him in the temple.

An Angel Announces Jesus' Birth

When Zechariah's wife Elizabeth was six months pregnant, her young cousin Mary had a very special visitor. An angel told Mary that she had been chosen to give birth to a special child, the Son of the Most High. Mary was betrothed (engaged) to a man named Joseph, who was from the family line of David.

Luke 1:26–56

THE BIRTH OF JESUS FORETOLD

[26] In the sixth month, God sent the angel Gabriel to Nazareth, a town in Galilee, [27] to a virgin pledged to be married to a man named Joseph, a descendant of David. The virgin's name was Mary. [28] The angel went to her and said, "Greetings, you who are highly favored! The Lord is with you."

[29] Mary was greatly troubled at his words and wondered what kind of greeting this might be. [30] But the angel said to her, "Do not be afraid, Mary, you have found favor with God. [31] You will be with child and give birth to a son, and you are to give him the name Jesus. [32] He will be great and will be called the Son of the Most High. The Lord God will give him the throne of his father David, [33] and he will reign over the house of Jacob forever; his kingdom will never end."

[34] "How will this be," Mary asked the angel, "since I am a virgin?"

[35] The angel answered, "The Holy Spirit will come upon you, and the power of the Most High will overshadow you. So the holy one to be born will be called[a] the Son of God. [36] Even Elizabeth your relative is going to have a child in her old age, and she who was said to be barren is in her sixth month. [37] For nothing is impossible with God."

[38] "I am the Lord's servant," Mary answered. "May it be to me as you have said." Then the angel left her.

MARY VISITS ELIZABETH

[39] At that time Mary got ready and hurried to a town in the hill country of Judea, [40] where she entered Zechariah's home and greeted Elizabeth. [41] When Elizabeth heard Mary's greeting, the baby leaped in her womb, and Elizabeth was filled with the Holy Spirit. [42] In a loud voice she exclaimed: "Blessed are you among women, and blessed is the child you will bear! [43] But why am I so favored, that the mother of my Lord should come to me? [44] As soon as the sound of your greeting reached my ears, the baby in my womb leaped for joy. [45] Blessed is she who has believed that what the Lord has said to her will be accomplished!"

MARY'S SONG

[46] And Mary said:

"My soul glorifies the Lord
[47]   and my spirit rejoices in God my Savior,
[48] for he has been mindful
        of the humble state of his servant.
    From now on all generations will call me blessed,

---

[a] 35 Or *So the child to be born will be called holy,*

⁴⁹   for the Mighty One has done great things for
            me —
        holy is his name.
⁵⁰ His mercy extends to those who fear him,
        from generation to generation.
⁵¹ He has performed mighty deeds with his arm;
        he has scattered those who are proud in their
            inmost thoughts.
⁵² He has brought down rulers from their thrones
        but has lifted up the humble.
⁵³ He has filled the hungry with good things
        but has sent the rich away empty.
⁵⁴ He has helped his servant Israel,
        remembering to be merciful
⁵⁵ to Abraham and his descendants forever,
        even as he said to our fathers."

⁵⁶ Mary stayed with Elizabeth for about three months
and then returned home.

JUST THE FACTS

1. What was the name of the angel who visited Mary? (v. 26)
2. What was the name Mary was to give her child? (v. 31)
3. What was Mary's final answer to the angel? (v. 38)

LET'S TALK

1. Why did Mary believe this very unusual announcement? Why did Mary visit Elizabeth?
2. What was Mary like? Why do you think God chose her to be Jesus' mother?

WHY THIS MATTERS

God showed that he can do the impossible — a virgin became pregnant by his Holy Spirit, and God's Son came into the world. Mary's song of praise in Luke 1:46–55 tells how wonderful this news is.

POINTS OF INTEREST

1:39–40 Mary's home in Nazareth was about 65 miles away from Jerusalem, where her cousin Elizabeth lived. In Bible times, that distance would have taken several days to travel. It was common for relatives to visit and stay for months at a time, like Mary did.

Joseph Has a Dream

Mary was promised to be married to Joseph. In those days betrothal, or engagement, was a very important legal agreement. But when Mary told Joseph she was pregnant, Joseph no longer wanted to marry her. Then he had a dream that convinced him that everything that had happened was from the Holy Spirit of God.

Matthew 1:18–25

THE BIRTH OF JESUS CHRIST

[18] This is how the birth of Jesus Christ came about: His mother Mary was pledged to be married to Joseph, but before they came together, she was found to be with child through the Holy Spirit. [19] Because Joseph her husband was a righteous man and did not want to expose her to public disgrace, he had in mind to divorce her quietly.

[20] But after he had considered this, an angel of the Lord appeared to him in a dream and said, "Joseph son of David, do not be afraid to take Mary home as your wife, because what is conceived in her is from the Holy Spirit. [21] She will give birth to a son, and you are to give him the name Jesus,[a] because he will save his people from their sins."

[22] All this took place to fulfill what the Lord had said through the prophet: [23] "The virgin will be with

---

[a] 21 *Jesus* is the Greek form of *Joshua*, which means *the LORD saves.*

child and will give birth to a son, and they will call him Immanuel"[a]—which means, "God with us."

²⁴When Joseph woke up, he did what the angel of the Lord had commanded him and took Mary home as his wife. ²⁵But he had no union with her until she gave birth to a son. And he gave him the name Jesus.

[a] *23* Isaiah 7:14

JUST THE FACTS

1. Who talked to Joseph in a dream? What did the messenger call Joseph? (v. 20)

2. What did the messenger tell Joseph would happen? (v. 21)

3. What was Joseph told to name the baby? Why? (v. 21)

LET'S TALK

1. How do you think Joseph felt after his dream? Have you ever had a dream that made you feel better about a situation?

2. Why is it important that these events took place according to the prophecy in verse 23?

WHY THIS MATTERS

God wanted Jesus, his own Son, to have both a father and a mother to care for him and bring him up according to the Law of Moses and the law of the land. God worked everything out to fulfill every detail prophesied by the prophets.

POINTS OF INTEREST

1:19 In Bible times, being betrothed meant the couple was legally promised to each other, but the bride didn't live with the bridegroom. After the wedding ceremony, the bride's family would have a big feast that lasted for six or seven days. Then the bride would go to live in her husband's house.

The Birth of John the Baptist

Zechariah and Elizabeth became the parents of John, just as the angel Gabriel had told Zechariah. Their son became the prophet who later announced the great news of the Messiah to the people of Israel and prepared them for Jesus' coming.

Luke 1:57-80

THE BIRTH OF JOHN THE BAPTIST

⁵⁷When it was time for Elizabeth to have her baby, she gave birth to a son. ⁵⁸Her neighbors and relatives heard that the Lord had shown her great mercy, and they shared her joy.

⁵⁹On the eighth day they came to circumcise the child, and they were going to name him after his father Zechariah, ⁶⁰but his mother spoke up and said, "No! He is to be called John."

⁶¹They said to her, "There is no one among your relatives who has that name."

⁶²Then they made signs to his father, to find out what he would like to name the child. ⁶³He asked for a writing tablet, and to everyone's astonishment he wrote, "His name is John." ⁶⁴Immediately his mouth was opened and his tongue was loosed, and he began to speak, praising God. ⁶⁵The neighbors were all filled with awe, and throughout the hill country of Judea people were talking about all these things. ⁶⁶Everyone who heard this wondered about it, asking, "What then is this child going to be?" For the Lord's hand was with him.

ZECHARIAH'S SONG

[67] His father Zechariah was filled with the Holy Spirit and prophesied:

[68] "Praise be to the Lord, the God of Israel,
>because he has come and has redeemed his
>>people.
[69] He has raised up a horn[a] of salvation for us
>in the house of his servant David
[70] (as he said through his holy prophets of long ago),
[71] salvation from our enemies
>and from the hand of all who hate us—
[72] to show mercy to our fathers
>and to remember his holy covenant,
[73] the oath he swore to our father Abraham:
[74] to rescue us from the hand of our enemies,
>and to enable us to serve him without fear
[75] in holiness and righteousness before him all
>>our days.

[76] And you, my child, will be called a prophet of
>the Most High;
>for you will go on before the Lord to prepare
>>the way for him,
[77] to give his people the knowledge of salvation
>through the forgiveness of their sins,
[78] because of the tender mercy of our God,
>by which the rising sun will come to us from
>>heaven
[79] to shine on those living in darkness
>and in the shadow of death,
>to guide our feet into the path of peace."

[80] And the child grew and became strong in spirit; and he lived in the desert until he appeared publicly to Israel.

---

[a] *69 Horn* here symbolizes strength.

JUST THE FACTS

1. What name did the people want Elizabeth to give her son? Why? (v. 59)

2. How was the baby's name finally chosen? (v. 63)

3. What happened to Zechariah when he wrote down the baby's name? (v. 64)

LET'S TALK

1. Names were very important during Bible times. They often told what the child meant to the parents or described who he or she would become. Why did your parents give you the name you have? Discuss the names of the people in your family and what they mean.

2. What do you suppose the people were actually saying when they were "talking about all these things" (v. 65)? What would you have talked about if you had heard something like this?

WHY THIS MATTERS

This story shows how much God loves us. He made sure that everything was ready for Jesus' birth by sending a messenger, John. God kept every promise he made and did the "impossible" to make it all happen just as he had said.

POINTS OF INTEREST

1:60 In Bible times, the mother often named a child. In the Old Testament, Leah, Rachel and Hannah named their children. A few times, someone else named a child: Pharaoh's daughter named Moses and the village women named Ruth's child Obed. Occasionally the father named a child or changed the name after the mother had selected one. That's why the people asked Zechariah what name he wanted for his son. He confirmed that the name of his son was John.

The Birth of Jesus

God had promised the people of Israel a Savior. Through the prophets, God had told them how the Savior would come and what he would do. All the things the prophets had said about Jesus' birth came to pass. Mary gave birth to Jesus in the town of Bethlehem, an ordinary, quiet place.

Luke 2:1-7

THE BIRTH OF JESUS

2 In those days Caesar Augustus issued a decree that a census should be taken of the entire Roman world. ²(This was the first census that took place while Quirinius was governor of Syria.) ³And everyone went to his own town to register.

⁴So Joseph also went up from the town of Nazareth in Galilee to Judea, to Bethlehem the town of David, because he belonged to the house and line of David. ⁵He went there to register with Mary, who was pledged to be married to him and was expecting a child. ⁶While they were there, the time came for the baby to be born, ⁷and she gave birth to her firstborn, a son. She wrapped him in cloths and placed him in a manger, because there was no room for them in the inn.

JUST THE FACTS

1. Why did Mary and Joseph go to Bethlehem? (vv. 1–3)
2. What was another name for the town of Bethlehem? (v. 4)
3. Why did Mary put the baby in a manger? (v. 7)

LET'S TALK

1. Can you think of some of the prophecies that were fulfilled when Jesus was born? Look back to the previous readings if you need to.
2. Why would God want his Son to be born in such a poor and ordinary place?

WHY THIS MATTERS

That night in Bethlehem, God came down to earth in the form of a little baby. God gave Jesus a humble beginning so that everyone could understand that he came to bring salvation to all people, even the poorest and lowliest. Jesus was born human, like us, so we could relate to him. He was God so that he could save us from our sins and give us new life.

POINTS OF INTEREST

2:7 The manger Mary laid Jesus in was a trough or open box used to hold grain or grasses to feed livestock. The area around Bethlehem has many limestone caves that were used in Bible times to shelter and feed animals. Although we think of a stable as a wooden building, the stable Jesus was born in may have been a cave located behind an inn.

The Shepherds and the Angels

Bethlehem was ordinarily a quiet town. But on the night that Jesus was born there, something happened outside of town — something spectacular!

Luke 2:8-20

THE SHEPHERDS AND THE ANGELS

⁸And there were shepherds living out in the fields nearby, keeping watch over their flocks at night. ⁹An angel of the Lord appeared to them, and the glory of the Lord shone around them, and they were terrified. ¹⁰But the angel said to them, "Do not be afraid. I bring you good news of great joy that will be for all the people. ¹¹Today in the town of David a Savior has been born to you; he is Christ*a* the Lord. ¹²This will be a sign to you: You will find a baby wrapped in cloths and lying in a manger."

¹³Suddenly a great company of the heavenly host appeared with the angel, praising God and saying,

¹⁴"Glory to God in the highest,
    and on earth peace to men on whom his favor
    rests."

¹⁵When the angels had left them and gone into heaven, the shepherds said to one another, "Let's go to Bethlehem and see this thing that has happened, which the Lord has told us about."

¹⁶So they hurried off and found Mary and Joseph,

a 11 Or *Messiah*. "The Christ" (Greek) and "the Messiah" (Hebrew) both mean "the Anointed One"; also in verse 26.

and the baby, who was lying in the manger. [17]When they had seen him, they spread the word concerning what had been told them about this child, [18]and all who heard it were amazed at what the shepherds said to them. [19]But Mary treasured up all these things and pondered them in her heart. [20]The shepherds returned, glorifying and praising God for all the things they had heard and seen, which were just as they had been told.

JUST THE FACTS

1. Who appeared to the shepherds out in the fields? (v. 9)

2. What did he say? (vv. 10–11)

3. What happened after this angel made his announcement? (v. 13)

LET'S TALK

1. Why were the shepherds terrified to see the angel and "the glory of the Lord"? (v. 9) How would you feel if you were camping out and saw this phenomenon?

2. What did the shepherds do after they went to see Jesus in the manger? Why?

WHY THIS MATTERS

The story of Jesus' birth had to be told, and the shepherds became witnesses to the indescribable miracle of the Messiah's coming. This story has amazed people for centuries, just as it amazed the shepherds and the people they told.

POINTS OF INTEREST

2:14 The hymn of the angels is called the "*Gloria in Excelsis Deo*," which is the refrain of the song "Angels We Have Heard on High" that we sing during the Christmas season. The phrase "Glory to God" praises the majesty of God, who dwells "in the highest" in heaven.

Mary and Joseph Present Jesus at the Temple

Forty days after his birth, Mary and Joseph took Jesus to the temple in Jerusalem. They were obeying religious laws that Moses had given the Israelites long before. They went to dedicate their firstborn son to God and to offer sacrifices.

Luke 2:21–40

JESUS PRESENTED IN THE TEMPLE

²¹On the eighth day, when it was time to circumcise him, he was named Jesus, the name the angel had given him before he had been conceived.

²²When the time of their purification according to the Law of Moses had been completed, Joseph and Mary took him to Jerusalem to present him to the Lord ²³(as it is written in the Law of the Lord, "Every firstborn male is to be consecrated to the Lord"[a]), ²⁴and to offer a sacrifice in keeping with what is said in the Law of the Lord: "a pair of doves or two young pigeons."[b]

²⁵Now there was a man in Jerusalem called Simeon, who was righteous and devout. He was waiting for the consolation of Israel, and the Holy Spirit was upon him. ²⁶It had been revealed to him by the Holy Spirit that he would not die before he had seen the Lord's Christ. ²⁷Moved by the Spirit, he went into the temple courts. When the parents brought in the child Jesus to do for

[a] 23 Exodus 13:2,12   [b] 24 Lev. 12:8

him what the custom of the Law required, [28]Simeon took him in his arms and praised God, saying:

[29]"Sovereign Lord, as you have promised,
    you now dismiss[a] your servant in peace.
[30]For my eyes have seen your salvation,
[31]   which you have prepared in the sight of all
        people,
[32]a light for revelation to the Gentiles
    and for glory to your people Israel."

[33]The child's father and mother marveled at what was said about him. [34]Then Simeon blessed them and said to Mary, his mother: "This child is destined to cause the falling and rising of many in Israel, and to be a sign that will be spoken against, [35]so that the thoughts of many hearts will be revealed. And a sword will pierce your own soul too."

[36]There was also a prophetess, Anna, the daughter of Phanuel, of the tribe of Asher. She was very old; she had lived with her husband seven years after her marriage, [37]and then was a widow until she was eighty-four.[b] She never left the temple but worshiped night and day, fasting and praying. [38]Coming up to them at that very moment, she gave thanks to God and spoke about the child to all who were looking forward to the redemption of Jerusalem.

[39]When Joseph and Mary had done everything required by the Law of the Lord, they returned to Galilee to their own town of Nazareth. [40]And the child grew and became strong; he was filled with wisdom, and the grace of God was upon him.

---

[a] 29 Or *promised, / now dismiss*   [b] 37 Or *widow for eighty-four years*

JUST THE FACTS

1. Why did Mary and Joseph go to Jerusalem?
   (vv. 22–24)

2. How did Mary and Joseph react to what Simeon said?
   (v. 33)

3. How old was Anna? What did she do every day?
   (v. 37)

LET'S TALK

1. How did Simeon's blessing confirm who Jesus was?
   Why did Mary and Joseph marvel at what was said
   about their son?

2. What were Simeon and Anna waiting for? What kind
   of people were they?

WHY THIS MATTERS

Simeon and Anna were faithful people with hearts that
were open to God. Even though Jesus was very young, it
was clear to Simeon and Anna that he was the Messiah
the Jewish people had been waiting and hoping for.

POINTS OF INTEREST

2:24 To observe the Law of Moses, a woman who had
given birth to a son was to wait 40 days; then she was
to sacrifice a lamb and either a dove or a pigeon. If a
woman could not afford to bring a lamb and a dove
or pigeon, she was allowed to bring two doves or two
pigeons.

The Visit of the Magi

Several months after Jesus was born, Magi (traditionally called wise men) came from the east to Jerusalem asking about a new king. First, they asked King Herod, who was a friend of the Roman rulers, where to find the one they were looking for. Then they traveled another five miles to the town where Jesus lived in order to find him.

Matthew 2:1-12

THE VISIT OF THE MAGI

2 After Jesus was born in Bethlehem in Judea, during the time of King Herod, Magi[a] from the east came to Jerusalem ²and asked, "Where is the one who has been born king of the Jews? We saw his star in the east[b] and have come to worship him."

³When King Herod heard this he was disturbed, and all Jerusalem with him. ⁴When he had called together all the people's chief priests and teachers of the law, he asked them where the Christ[c] was to be born. ⁵"In Bethlehem in Judea," they replied, "for this is what the prophet has written:

⁶"'But you, Bethlehem, in the land of Judah,
    are by no means least among the rulers of
        Judah;
for out of you will come a ruler
    who will be the shepherd of my people Israel.'[d]"

[a] 1 Traditionally *Wise Men*   [b] 2 Or *star when it rose*
[c] 4 Or *Messiah*   [d] 6 Micah 5:2

⁷Then Herod called the Magi secretly and found out from them the exact time the star had appeared. ⁸He sent them to Bethlehem and said, "Go and make a careful search for the child. As soon as you find him, report to me, so that I too may go and worship him."

⁹After they had heard the king, they went on their way, and the star they had seen in the east*a* went ahead of them until it stopped over the place where the child was. ¹⁰When they saw the star, they were overjoyed. ¹¹On coming to the house, they saw the child with his mother Mary, and they bowed down and worshiped him. Then they opened their treasures and presented him with gifts of gold and of incense and of myrrh. ¹²And having been warned in a dream not to go back to Herod, they returned to their country by another route.

a 9 Or *seen when it rose*

JUST THE FACTS

1. Whom did the Magi say they were looking for? (v. 2)

2. What was the name of the king who was disturbed when he heard of another king being born? (v. 3)

3. What did the Magi do when they found Mary with her child? (v. 11)

LET'S TALK

1. Why was King Herod disturbed when he heard that the Messiah had been born? What did he think the Messiah would do?

2. Why do you think the Magi didn't go back to King Herod?

WHY THIS MATTERS

The Magi were the first to acknowledge Jesus as a king. This affirmed what the angel had said to Mary: Jesus would receive the throne of David, and his kingdom would have no end (see Luke 1:32–33).

POINTS OF INTEREST

2:2 Astronomers have explained that the star of Bethlehem was a comet, a nova or an alignment of Jupiter, Saturn and Mars. But history does not record that anyone besides the Magi saw this star. Apparently the star was a celestial phenomena God created just for this occasion.

Jesus, the Son of God, Is Baptized

When John grew up, he traveled from place to place telling people that the Messiah was coming and that they should change their ways. He did this to prepare them for the Messiah. Then he baptized them in the river to show that their hearts were clean. One day, Jesus came to be baptized too.

Matthew 3:13–17

THE BAPTISM OF JESUS

¹³Then Jesus came from Galilee to the Jordan to be baptized by John. ¹⁴But John tried to deter him, saying, "I need to be baptized by you, and do you come to me?"

¹⁵Jesus replied, "Let it be so now; it is proper for us to do this to fulfill all righteousness." Then John consented.

¹⁶As soon as Jesus was baptized, he went up out of the water. At that moment heaven was opened, and he saw the Spirit of God descending like a dove and lighting on him. ¹⁷And a voice from heaven said, "This is my Son, whom I love; with him I am well pleased."

JUST THE FACTS

1. What did John say to Jesus when Jesus came to be baptized? (v. 14)
2. What happened when Jesus came out of the water? (v. 16)
3. What did the voice from heaven say? (v. 17)

LET'S TALK

1. Jesus never sinned. So why did the Holy Spirit need to come down on him?
2. Why do you think it was important that God made this announcement?

WHY THIS MATTERS

The baptism of Jesus was the beginning of Jesus' work on earth. The Holy Spirit came down to give him the power to do miracles and heal people, to teach, and to do all the other things he came to do. God called Jesus his Son, encouraging him and announcing to everyone that he was the Messiah.

POINTS OF INTEREST

3:13 The Jordan River runs north to south from the Sea of Galilee to the Dead Sea. The distance between the two seas is 65 miles, but the Jordan, because it winds its way south, is actually 135 miles long. Before modern times, the Jordan was about 100 feet wide and three to ten feet deep, except when heavy rains in winter and spring caused it to flood.

From the Beginning

The Gospel of John tells us that the "word" is not only the spoken word (the message from God and Jesus' teachings) but also the "Word," Jesus, the actual person of God himself in Christ. He is the living expression of God's presence with his people.

John 1:1-18

THE WORD BECAME FLESH

1 In the beginning was the Word, and the Word was with God, and the Word was God. ²He was with God in the beginning.

³Through him all things were made; without him nothing was made that has been made. ⁴In him was life, and that life was the light of men. ⁵The light shines in the darkness, but the darkness has not understood[a] it.

⁶There came a man who was sent from God; his name was John. ⁷He came as a witness to testify concerning that light, so that through him all men might believe. ⁸He himself was not the light; he came only as a witness to the light. ⁹The true light that gives light to every man was coming into the world.[b]

¹⁰He was in the world, and though the world was

---

[a] 5 Or *darkness, and the darkness has not overcome*   [b] 9 Or *This was the true light that gives light to every man who comes into the world*

made through him, the world did not recognize him. ¹¹He came to that which was his own, but his own did not receive him. ¹²Yet to all who received him, to those who believed in his name, he gave the right to become children of God— ¹³children born not of natural descent,[a] nor of human decision or a husband's will, but born of God.

¹⁴The Word became flesh and made his dwelling among us. We have seen his glory, the glory of the One and Only,[b] who came from the Father, full of grace and truth.

¹⁵John testifies concerning him. He cries out, saying, "This was he of whom I said, 'He who comes after me has surpassed me because he was before me.'" ¹⁶From the fullness of his grace we have all received one blessing after another. ¹⁷For the law was given through Moses; grace and truth came through Jesus Christ. ¹⁸No one has ever seen God, but God the One and Only,[b,c] who is at the Father's side, has made him known.

---

[a] 13 Greek *of bloods*   [b] 14 Or *the Only Begotten*   [c] 18 Some manuscripts *but the only* (or *only begotten*) *Son*

JUST THE FACTS

1. Who was in the beginning? (v. 1)

2. Whom did God send to tell about the "light"? (vv. 6–8)

3. What was given through Moses? What came through Christ? (v. 17)

LET'S TALK

1. What is grace? What are some of the blessings you have received because of God's grace?

2. What did the writer John mean by "darkness" and "light"? (vv. 4–5)

WHY THIS MATTERS

Long before the world began, God planned to send Jesus to live among people on earth. Through Jesus, God has shown us his glory.

POINTS OF INTEREST

1:4–5 Throughout the Bible, "light" is linked with God's majesty, glory and goodness, while "darkness" is linked with Satan and evil. John used these word pictures several times in this Gospel and in his letters.

God's Great Gift of Love

A Pharisee named Nicodemus came at night to ask Jesus who he was. Jesus told Nicodemus why he had come from God and what he was sent to do. Then Jesus told Nicodemus that Nicodemus would have to be "born again" of the Spirit. In a few sentences, Jesus summed up the Good News.

John 3:1–21

JESUS TEACHES NICODEMUS

3 Now there was a man of the Pharisees named Nicodemus, a member of the Jewish ruling council. ²He came to Jesus at night and said, "Rabbi, we know you are a teacher who has come from God. For no one could perform the miraculous signs you are doing if God were not with him."

³In reply Jesus declared, "I tell you the truth, no one can see the kingdom of God unless he is born again.ᵃ"

⁴"How can a man be born when he is old?" Nicodemus asked. "Surely he cannot enter a second time into his mother's womb to be born!"

⁵Jesus answered, "I tell you the truth, no one can enter the kingdom of God unless he is born of water and the Spirit. ⁶Flesh gives birth to flesh, but the Spiritᵇ gives birth to spirit. ⁷You should not be surprised at my saying, 'Youᶜ must be born again.' ⁸The wind blows

---

ᵃ 3 Or *born from above*; also in verse 7   ᵇ 6 Or *but spirit*
ᶜ 7 The Greek is plural.

wherever it pleases. You hear its sound, but you cannot tell where it comes from or where it is going. So it is with everyone born of the Spirit."

⁹"How can this be?" Nicodemus asked.

¹⁰"You are Israel's teacher," said Jesus, "and do you not understand these things? ¹¹I tell you the truth, we speak of what we know, and we testify to what we have seen, but still you people do not accept our testimony. ¹²I have spoken to you of earthly things and you do not believe; how then will you believe if I speak of heavenly things? ¹³No one has ever gone into heaven except the one who came from heaven—the Son of Man.ᵃ ¹⁴Just as Moses lifted up the snake in the desert, so the Son of Man must be lifted up, ¹⁵that everyone who believes in him may have eternal life.ᵇ

¹⁶"For God so loved the world that he gave his one and only Son,ᶜ that whoever believes in him shall not perish but have eternal life. ¹⁷For God did not send his Son into the world to condemn the world, but to save the world through him. ¹⁸Whoever believes in him is not condemned, but whoever does not believe stands condemned already because he has not believed in the name of God's one and only Son.ᵈ ¹⁹This is the verdict: Light has come into the world, but men loved darkness instead of light because their deeds were evil. ²⁰Everyone who does evil hates the light, and will not come into the light for fear that his deeds will be exposed. ²¹But whoever lives by the truth comes into the light, so that it may be seen plainly that what he has done has been done through God."ᵉ

ᵃ 13 Some manuscripts *Man, who is in heaven*   ᵇ 15 Or *believes may have eternal life in him*   ᶜ 16 Or *his only begotten Son*
ᵈ 18 Or *God's only begotten Son*   ᵉ 21 Some interpreters end the quotation after verse 15.

JUST THE FACTS

1. What do people have to do in order to have eternal life? (v. 16)
2. Why did God send his Son into the world? (v. 17)
3. Why do people love the darkness more than the light? (vv. 19–20)

LET'S TALK

1. Verse 16 tells us what people have to do to have eternal life. What does it mean to "believe"? Why is this Good News so difficult for some people to understand?
2. What do we have to do to live by "the truth"? (v. 21) What does living by the truth look like?

WHY THIS MATTERS

The reason Jesus came to earth, lived and taught among people, and died for our sins is because "God so loved the world" (v. 16). Jesus is God's great gift of love to each and every one of us.

POINTS OF INTEREST

3:14 When Jesus talked about Moses lifting up the snake in the desert, he was referring to the time the Israelites complained about the food God had provided for them. God sent poisonous snakes into the camp to punish the people. Some people were saved from death by looking up at a bronze snake that God had told Moses to make and place on a pole.

Jesus Christ Is Supreme

Many years after Isaiah and Micah prophesied about Jesus the Messiah, the apostle Paul wrote a letter to the church at Colosse to tell them that Jesus was both God and a human being. Paul included this beautiful hymn in praise of the glory and supremacy of Christ.

Colossians 1:15 – 20

THE SUPREMACY OF CHRIST

[15] He is the image of the invisible God, the firstborn over all creation. [16] For by him all things were created: things in heaven and on earth, visible and invisible, whether thrones or powers or rulers or authorities; all things were created by him and for him. [17] He is before all things, and in him all things hold together. [18] And he is the head of the body, the church; he is the beginning and the firstborn from among the dead, so that in everything he might have the supremacy. [19] For God was pleased to have all his fullness dwell in him, [20] and through him to reconcile to himself all things, whether things on earth or things in heaven, by making peace through his blood, shed on the cross.

JUST THE FACTS

1. Paul said that Jesus Christ is the "firstborn." (v. 15) Of what is he the firstborn?

2. What did Jesus Christ create? (v. 16)

3. Of what is Jesus Christ the head? (v. 18)

LET'S TALK

1. What does it mean that Jesus Christ is the "image of the invisible God"? (v. 15)

2. What do you think Paul meant when he said that in Jesus Christ "all things hold together"? (v. 17)

WHY THIS MATTERS

Jesus was born in a small town and lived among common people like us, but Paul gives us the bigger picture of who Christ really is and what Christ has done for us.

POINTS OF INTEREST

1:19 In Paul's day, some people taught that matter — anything you could taste, see or touch — was evil, so the human body was evil. They said a person's spirit was "trapped" in an evil body and could escape only by some secret knowledge. So they said Jesus couldn't be both God and man because he lived in a body.

"Let All God's Angels Worship Him"

The author of the book of Hebrews, who did not identify himself, wrote this letter to Jewish Christians to encourage them in their faith. He reminded them that Jesus Christ came to the earth to fulfill the Old Testament Scriptures, that he is God, and that he is greater than even the angels.

Hebrews 1:1-14

THE SON SUPERIOR TO ANGELS

1 In the past God spoke to our forefathers through the prophets at many times and in various ways, ²but in these last days he has spoken to us by his Son, whom he appointed heir of all things, and through whom he made the universe. ³The Son is the radiance of God's glory and the exact representation of his being, sustaining all things by his powerful word. After he had provided purification for sins, he sat down at the right hand of the Majesty in heaven. ⁴So he became as much superior to the angels as the name he has inherited is superior to theirs.

⁵For to which of the angels did God ever say,

"You are my Son;
today I have become your Father[a]"[b]?

Or again,

"I will be his Father,

[a] 5 Or *have begotten you*   [b] 5 Psalm 2:7   [c] 5 2 Samuel 7:14; 1 Chron. 17:13

and he will be my Son"*c*?

⁶And again, when God brings his firstborn into the world, he says,

"Let all God's angels worship him."*a*

⁷In speaking of the angels he says,

"He makes his angels winds,
  his servants flames of fire."*b*

⁸But about the Son he says,

"Your throne, O God, will last for ever and ever,
  and righteousness will be the scepter of your
    kingdom.
⁹You have loved righteousness and hated wickedness;
  therefore God, your God, has set you above
    your companions
by anointing you with the oil of joy."*c*

¹⁰He also says,

"In the beginning, O Lord, you laid the
    foundations of the earth,
  and the heavens are the work of your hands.
¹¹They will perish, but you remain;
  they will all wear out like a garment.
¹²You will roll them up like a robe;
  like a garment they will be changed.
But you remain the same,
  and your years will never end."*d*

¹³To which of the angels did God ever say,

"Sit at my right hand
until I make your enemies
  a footstool for your feet"*e*?

---

^a *6* Deut. 32:43 (see Dead Sea Scrolls and Septuagint)
^b *7* Psalm 104:4   ^c *9* Psalm 45:6,7   ^d *12* Psalm 102:25-27
^e *13* Psalm 110:1

¹⁴Are not all angels ministering spirits sent to serve those who will inherit salvation?

JUST THE FACTS

1. How did God speak to "our forefathers"? How does God speak "in these last days"? (vv. 1–2)

2. Where does the Son now sit? (v. 3)

3. What tasks has God given the angels? (vv. 6–7,14)

LET'S TALK

1. What words and phrases show how Christ is greater than the angels?

2. How does this reading help you understand the "big picture" of Jesus' coming?

WHY THIS MATTERS

The Messiah's coming was foretold by the prophets. Jesus was born and lived and died as a human being. Now Jesus Christ holds a position of honor in heaven at the right hand of God.

POINTS OF INTEREST

1:5 The author of this letter quoted two Old Testament texts that his original readers would have been familiar with — Psalm 2:7 and 2 Samuel 7:14 — to prove that Jesus Christ is God's Son.

The Family Reading Bible

If you've enjoyed the Christmas Story, consider exploring the complete Bible with your entire family. *The Family Reading* 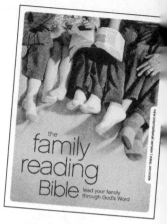 *Bible* provides a roadmap full of insightful and engaging questions and fun facts designed for you — a Christian parent looking for a way to read and explore the Bible together with your kids. With three easy-to-use reading tracks to accommodate children of any age, *The NIV Family Reading Bible* will nurture your kids' interest in God's Word.

Hardcover Edition: 978-0-310-94196-5

Pick up a copy at your favorite bookstore or online!